Being a Better Me for Me

Sparkle Lindsay

SPARKLE

Zanzara Press
918 5th Street
Ames, IA 50010
USA

zanzarapress.com

editor@zanzarapress.com

For more information, please address
editor@zanzarapress.com

ISBN: 978-1-941892-48-0

Cover design and interior layout © 2021 polytekton

Introduction

I have had to fight to take my life back, and in doing so, I found that it is important to enjoy a little bit of sunshine each day. I felt compelled to share with you a pocket guide that shows you quick tips and tricks to be better for you daily. At times we can make things so hard, when all we really need is to open our hearts, our minds, and speak our truth. I hope you enjoy this book in its entirety. You can take it anywhere you need to go, while allowing things to be what they are going to be. Give yourself permission to open your mind to the power behind these words, and use them to your advantage, for you alone deserve it.

Table of Contents

When you slow down and you deepen your breath, you are letting your body know that it's okay to trust the present moment.

Write down five things you're grateful for and keep them in your pocket. When anxiety and/or chaos sets in, pull these out of your pocket and read them to yourself.

Don't let other's judgment distract you from your greatness. Embrace it, believe in yourself, because it's just the beginning.

Give yourself positive affirmations throughout the day. An example would be: I am beautiful, smart, willing, determined; then, also, tell yourself positive affirmations you intend to be. Examples are: I am deserving of, I am entitled to, I am capable of, I believe I am worthy of transformation.

*Your emotions don't define you, for
they are temporary, not permanent.*

Pull a feelings list from Google; this will help you work on better ways to describe how you are feeling at any given moment. We all know that checking in with ourselves is the first prescription to success.

The best preparation for tomorrow comes from doing your best today.

Before bedtime write down three positive things you did that day, big or small, and read them to yourself. Place them under your pillow, or at your bedside. When you wake up in the morning, read them to yourself again to remind you of the amazing day you had and how accomplished you were. This will help put you in a positive mindset for the day ahead.

*Just as a gardener tends to their flowers,
care for your practice daily and watch
it grow, strengthen, and blossom.*

Practice the essentials of daily life.
Maybe take some classes or courses on
effective listening, communication,
patience, resilience, determination, etc.

Sometimes, the most important
thing in a whole day is the rest we
take between two deep breaths.

Write a list of self-care acts you love
to do just for you: meditate, pray,
talk, read, journal, color, draw, walk,
workout, paint, roller-skate, make
videos, play cards, sing, dance, play
video games, have coffee with friends,
etc. DO SOMETHING!

When everything is moving and shifting, the best way to counteract chaos is stillness. Be still.

Hold space for yourself, give yourself alone time, focus on the Gift of Being, and you'll begin to experience why being with yourself is needed.

*The day you plant the seed is not
the day you eat the fruit.*

Find a favorite saying or a prayer of your liking, and break it down; be curious about what it means to you.

No. It is a full and complete sentence.

Internal and external boundaries. Do you have them?

Miscommunication is a natural part of communication.

When having a conversation with people, focus on acknowledging and validating the topic along with its contents, as well as finding compassion for yourself and others, as you work your way through it together.

Notes

9 781941 892480